# ideas

{
**101 GREAT IDEAS**
for *increasing* your
visibility, credibility and profitability
}

Matt Schoenherr
(Business Activist)

**DREAMSCAPE**
MULTIMEDIA

# ideas

Cover and book design by Matt Schoenherr.
Author photos by Diana Liang.

**DREAMSCAPE**
MULTIMEDIA

Published by
Dreamscape Multimedia
120 N. Washington Square, Suite 805
Lansing, MI 48933

The author may be contacted at the following address:

Dreamscape Multimedia
120 N. Washington Square, Suite 805
Lansing, MI 48933
phone: 517.394.3000, fax: 517.394.3000
e-mail: ideas@dreamscapemultimedia.com
website: www.dreamscapemultimedia.com

Printed in the United States of America

First Printing: October 2010

ISBN 978-0-615-40257-4

Dedicated to my wife, Kelly (a.k.a. Grace,) and to our four beautiful children, Gabriel, Sovereign, Natalia, and Canon.

And to Divinity for bringing these awesome teachers into my life.

# Contents

# Introduction

The purpose of this book is to help business owners and nonprofits—from the one-person show to the marketing department of the large corporations—with the magic of marketing: the creative ideas.

*Ideas* was built to collect the wealth of creative solutions others have used successfully and offer them as an alternative to paying large amounts of money to professional marketing firms.

Certainly, face-to-face, professional expertise can't be totally replaced, but it is my intent to place creativity and proven ideas into your hands at a reasonable cost. *Ideas* offers you a beginning—a starting point. It will not do the marketing for you, but it will help you build your game plan.

Within this book, you will find real solutions to the marketing mystery. Some are simple, while others are more complex. Some ideas you can implement for free, while others will cost money. Regardless of which ideas you use, remember that all of them merit consideration.

As a client told me once, "Sometimes, all it takes is one good idea."

In support of your efforts,

Matt

# STRATEGY

**It might seem obvious, but all marketing efforts should begin with a focused plan.** Yet so many business owners and nonprofit directors don't have one. Why? It takes work! There can be a lot to look at when developing a comprehensive marketing plan. Competitive analysis, market research, distribution plans, target market, SWOT (Strengths, Weaknesses, Opportunities, and Threats) analysis, branding, positioning, and your marketing mix (channels of choice) are all things that may be considered. Of course, this part of the strategizing is all very technical and scientific (even though most of it will be distilled down into a best guess). This section addresses a mixture of the science and the magic involved in approaching your marketing efforts.

# Idea #1

**Mark in your calendar a time each day to market yourself.** Even as little as fifteen minutes a day of pure focus on marketing activities will offer returns.

**Variation:** Instead of a mere fifteen minutes, set aside an hour a day for either yourself or a member of your staff to work on marketing activities.

# Idea #2

**Set aside money for marketing efforts each year.** Don't use it for anything else. Often, we have a tendency to pull our marketing funds from the same pool of money as our operating funds. This habit can reduce an organization's ability to market itself when the time is right. Be especially protective of your marketing budget; it is this investment that pays the bills.

# Idea #3

**Create a marketing calendar.** List marketing opportunities you'll have throughout the year so you know what you have coming up and can plan your time and resources accordingly. (Be sure to place key event reminders in your calendar so you'll be aware of the approaching events in plenty of time.)

# Idea #4

You probably already have ideas and future plans for your company in your head. **Put these ideas down in print somewhere.** Include a section for collecting marketing ideas and opportunity information. You'll be amazed at the great ideas you lose track of as you get caught up in your day-to-day efforts.

# Idea #5

**In the client database you should already be maintaining, track who ordered what service or product and when.** This will assist you when you reach out to those customers again. With this knowledge, you will have a better understanding of what they do as well as what has been important to them in the past. More important, you will be gaining a picture about who buys from you and why.

# Idea #6

**In your weekly, monthly, or quarterly e-newsletter, don't place entire articles.** Instead, place only the first few sentences—just enough to generate interest and give an idea about the content. Then, place a link back to your website, where they can continue reading the entire article.

**Explanation:** This serves two purposes. First, you're able to save your precious newsletter real estate for packing in more articles, news, or offers. Second, you'll be able to track the interest in each article (and therefore, each topic being presented) as people click through to your site.

# Idea #7

**Use humor in regard to your product or service.** Poke fun at yourself and get your message across at the same time.

**Example:** Dental offices are famous for providing dental floss during Halloween trick-or-treating fun. Instead, why not send your clients fake hillbilly teeth as a reminder to maintain good dental hygiene during sweet holidays? For promotional thrust, have your office's logo and contact info printed on any giveaways.

# Idea #8

**Make sure your customers can order from you online.** If they can't order from you online, make sure they can order by phone or by fax. You're in the business of making it easier for your customers to do business with you! Your challenge is to analyze how easy it is for customers to get what they want from you. Have you ever tried to buy something from yourself? Go through the process. Have your staff go through the process. Survey your customers; how did they feel about their first experience with you? Compile your notes and discuss your findings. Then, fix what's broken.

# Idea #9

**Offer to match your competition's prices.** Bargain shoppers thrive on being able to bring in your competition's ads to have you beat the prices. There are a few things that work to your advantage here:

- ☑ Your regular patrons will be less likely to be swayed away from you because of price.

- ☑ The hunt for the lowest price is a process that engages the public and draws attention.

- ☑ You never have to worry about keeping a tab on the competition's price strategy (but you do have to worry about being able to maintain the same price strategy).

# Idea #10

**Seek out your competition, and look for opportunities to play off each other's strengths.** In making your competition strategic partners, you will be adding to the repertoire of products and services you are able to offer your customers. You may seek special pricing or a commission for driving business to one another, but ultimately, your goal is to help the customer.

# Idea #11

**Tell your story.** Oftentimes, in our attempt to be consummate professionals, we are leery of telling our story (why you do what you do, what makes you tick, what ticks you off, and so on). As any seasoned public speaker will tell you, stories have a way of intimating us with our audience. A good story can work wonders for an ailing brand.

**Tip:** A good story is often sacrificed in lieu of political correctness, making it stale and dull. You can help your employees tell those inspiring, slightly off-center stories by encouraging a culture that assumes the best intent.

**Example:** Family values win. By the cash register, the store owners show a picture of their three beautiful children grinning at the customer. Below is a handwritten note that says, *This is why our hours are what they are.* The story is brief and clear, tells the customer about the values of the owners, and inspires loyalty through this intimacy.

How can you accomplish the same through use of story?

# Idea #12

**Why is it, in this day and age, that there are still some stores and restaurants that don't accept credit or debit cards?** This is the epitome of making it difficult for your customers to do business with you. There is nothing worse than to make it through an entire meal, only to discover the place only accepts cash. At this point, you will either end up washing dishes or hunting around the neighborhood for an ATM. This is ridiculous. If you're in business, find a way to accept credit cards. Expanding your ability to collect on funds immediately will pay dividends in the long run.

**Tip:** Some entrepreneurs are deterred from processing credit cards because of things like a 3 percent processing fee, monthly gateway fees, and so on. Here's a reality check: I once had a client ask me if he could pay his installment for web design services with a credit card. The payment, the second of four, would have been over $1,000, which was a lot of money for me at the time. I had only begun that week considering the notion of accepting credit cards, so I told the client I had to decline the offer and wait for the check. "The check is in the mail," the client said.

Well, that check never arrived. Turns out, that would have been the last payment I would have received from him, as his business folded in the weeks to come.

Still concerned about the additional monthly cost of accepting credit cards? A small raise in your rate or your prices will cover the cost. Look at the nature of your business. If you are in retail, offer high-ticket items, or have the need for recurring billing due to subscriptions, memberships, or regular donations, you are a good candidate to accept credit cards.

# Ideas #13–17

**One of the best ways to stay in front of your audience or market is to provide value first.** One of the best ways to provide this value is to deliver great information, especially important in today's information-based society. Pulling together information and knowledge for people accomplishes a few things:

- ☑ First, it helps you clarify your thoughts. Taking even a small amount of time to write on matters important to your industry will greatly assist you in those instances where you're called upon to speak on such topics.

- ☑ Secondly, in providing useful information to others, you make yourself a resource, which is paramount in gaining credibility.

- ☑ Third, in writing or compiling information, you are furthering your own education.

**Examples:** Here are a number of ways you might deliver valuable information to others:

- ♀ **#13: Write an instructional brochure.**

- ♀ **#14: Start a quarterly, monthly, or weekly newsletter.**

- ♀ **#15: Submit an article to local newspapers or business magazines.**

- ♀ **#16: Produce and distribute an audio or video presentation on a topic in your industry.** Deliver this valuable information through an interactive CD or via the Internet.

- ♀ **#17: Publish a book.**

## Idea #18

**Create a referral program.** (Read: Make it worth other people's time to help you reach new clients.) The goal of a referral program is to create revenue or to provide some other incentive for those who help you reach more people.

Example: Dreamscape Multimedia offers a referral program with our web hosting service and makes it free to sign up using a simple one-page form. We call it our Prosperity program, as it pays a hefty 50 percent monthly commission* on any active hosting accounts you refer to us.

*Giving back 50 percent of a revenue stream may not be possible for your company. Determine what a responsible return might look like, and proceed conservatively at first.

# COMMUNITY INVOLVEMENT

**What are you doing to assist your local, national, or international community?** How are you getting involved, and how are you giving back? Community involvement is typically something that requires more of your time but less of your capital, so if you're operating on a budget, these ideas are for you. Begin by asking yourself the question, "How can I help?" Then, pick the lucky cause, charity, board, or group, and begin helping as an ambassador of your organization. Maybe you help out with an annual event. Maybe you have something to offer by volunteering your time, energy, and talents on a regular basis. Whatever effort you choose to support, make sure you believe in the cause before you commit to it.

# Idea #19

**Hone your public-speaking skills.** Join Toastmasters (www.toastmasters.org). As you move onward and upward into the business community, you will be called upon to give presentations before groups (one of the best ways to be perceived as an authority on your topic). Being proficient and persuasive in communicating ideas and stories before an audience is a huge asset. If you're petrified by the thought of public speaking, take solace: The point isn't to get rid of the butterflies, it's to get them flying in formation.

# Idea #20

**Donate your products or services to a charity auction.** In doing so, you add value to the fundraiser while promoting yourself. Furthermore, the fact you're willing to offer your time for a good cause can only help your own cause, and you just might be helping someone who wouldn't have been able to afford your services otherwise.

**Tip:** Get started by contacting your local radio stations, libraries, or newspapers. You might also do a search online for charity auctions in your area.

# Idea #21

**Be one of the speakers at your local high school on Career Day.** This gets you practice in front of what could be a tough group. (If you can keep their attention and inspire them, you can approach any audience.) Be sure to research the school first. Have they won any big games lately? What sport season are they in? What are the students focused on? What are their challenges? How can you make your own story something they can relate to?

**Remember:** Your audience isn't limited to the students; it includes their parents and the school faculty.

# Idea #22

**If you are aware of an annual conference in your industry, offer to be a panelist.** If it's too late for this year's conference, contact the event coordinators and voice your interest in attending next year's conference. Anytime you're able to present valuable ideas on your topic of specialty, you bring value to the effort of marketing yourself as an authority.

**Tip:** Nervous speaking in front of groups? Join Toastmasters to sharpen your public-speaking skills.

# Idea #23

**Teach a class at your local community college.** For as little as one or two nights a week, take a few hours and guide a class through the curriculum of your specialty. Students want real-world information from someone who is spending most of his time in the trenches. Bring your successes and failures to them. Let them learn from your experience—and place another feather in your marketing cap while you're doing it.

# Idea #24

**Volunteer for a local nonprofit group or charity.**
Maybe you have something to offer by volunteering on an advisory board. Whatever direction you choose, be sure your efforts are a reflection of the values you hold close to your heart. The cause you support must inspire you on a deep, personal level. Otherwise, you will tire quickly and may end up abandoning the effort before you've even begun—and that is *not* the way to build a reputation for quality.

# NETWORKING

The current statistics for cold-calling success rates state that for every one hundred cold calls you make, you can expect about three appointments, out of which you might score one sale. Does this sound like an efficient use of your time? **Networking is the art of connection. It is the starting point in the relationship-building process**. In its simplest form, networking is a subtle, soft-sell approach to marketing. In its most powerful form, it is a means of building a very efficient, highly proactive team of partners who can provide you with an endless flow of referrals. People do business with people they know, like, and trust. The first of those criteria is to know you. This is why we network.

# Idea #25

**Always have enough business cards with you.** While this seems like it should be obvious, people are still caught off-guard without their business cards. You'll never know when or where opportunities will arise. Also, whenever you know you're on your way to a trade show, mixer, or other networking event, make sure you take a lot of business cards. It's better to have too many than not enough!


**Tip:** Keep a number of "card caches" around you at all times. Keeping business cards in your car, at your desk, at your home office, and in your briefcase or purse can keep you from looking ill-prepared if you forget to replenish the cards in your wallet.

# Ideas #26–29

**Here are some tips for dealing with name tags:**

💡 **#26: Go above and beyond the paper name tags you have to wear at many events.** Be prepared with your own professional name tag, complete with company logo. They're inexpensive and stand out in a crowd. Have two or three made, and keep one in your car at all times.

💡 **#27: Name tags with magnet backs instead of pins are easier on your suits.** Most promotional products companies can have them made for you.

💡 **#28: You really only need your first name (printed in big letters) on a name tag.** Upon meeting you for the first time, people only need to concern themselves with your first name. If they're interested in meeting with you after your initial introduction, they'll find your last name on your business card.

💡 **#29: Name Tag Feng Shui:** Place your name tag on your right side instead of your left. When you shake someone's hand, your name will be closer to his eyes.

# Idea #30

**Join a networking and referral group** like Local Business Network (LBN) or Business Networking International (BNI). This may also take the form of joining a local business association, rotary, or other similar group. Joining these groups offers you an opportunity to meet and network with other small-business owners in the spirit of bringing opportunity to one another. By getting to know your fellow entrepreneurs, you broaden your personal network—and therefore the value you bring to your prospects and clients through your ability to refer problem-solvers to them—while maintaining a finger on the pulse of the local market.

**Tip:** These groups can be wonderful sources of referrals, as well as training in the world of business-to-business relationship building.

**Tip:** Websites like Meetup.com and LinkedIn.com can also be a great source for meeting and networking with local entrepreneurs.

# Idea #31

**Know your neighbors.** Especially in a retail environment, it is important that retailers work together to synchronize and support each other's activities. Likewise, the same can be true of strategic partners, where physical location isn't as important as reciprocal efforts. If you haven't taken the time to meet your neighbors (e.g., the businesses on your block, in your complex, in your part of town), you're missing out on a great opportunity. Building relationships with these folks will lead to the ability to refer business to them, as well as the opportunity to receive referred business from them.

# Ideas #32–37

**You've arrived at the latest networking event.** You have your name tag. You have your drink. You're looking sharp. Now what?

If you arrived at the event with someone else, you shouldn't be standing around talking to that person all night. You're there to make new connections.

> ♀ **#32: Don't be afraid to smile, extend your hand, and introduce yourself.** This is why you're here: to meet people.

**Trick:** If you don't know anyone, stand in the food or bar line. This way, you'll always have at least two people to talk to: the one in front of you and the one behind you.

> ♀ **#33: Don't interrupt a conversation.** Not only will this create a poor first impression, but everything you say after that will be received at a deficit. Instead, stand close, and when a pause presents itself, ease into the conversation gracefully.

> ♀ **#34: You have two ears and one mouth. Use them proportionately.** It's about them, not you. Ask about them and show a sincere interest. "They don't care what

you have to say, until they know that you care." —Zig Ziglar

💡 **#35: Ask smart questions.** Listen and learn. Prepare several qualifying questions before going to a networking event. If you find a prospect, qualify him before arranging a follow-up.

💡 **#36: When it's your turn to talk, be brief but succinct and powerful.** You must be able to present your case in sixty seconds or less. This may include who you are, what you do, what benefits you offer customers, and why you are better than the competition.

💡 **#37: Be enthusiastic and positive.** People don't want to hear you complain about your day, your boss, or your lot in life. (Save that for your spouse, therapist, or best friend.) People enjoy working with positive people.

**Remember:** Your goal at a networking event is to meet as many people as possible, qualify them, and arrange appropriate follow-up. Sell yourself first, and then your products and services.

# ATMOSPHERE

**How can you invest in your atmosphere?** This might be a fresh coat of paint, displaying artwork from local artists, or selecting music appropriate to your brand. People will pay more for the experience. For example, in blind taste tests, most folks have chosen Dunkin' Donuts versus Starbucks coffee. Dunkin' Donuts coffee goes for about ninety-seven cents per cup. Starbucks sells its coffee for four dollars, but it also provides its patrons with a warm atmosphere, hip music, and the luxury of wireless Internet access, and in doing so, it creates a meeting place. People will pay for the atmosphere, the experience—the opportunity to belong to a cool culture.

# Idea #38

**There is no better way to let your customers know you're struggling than to keep the temperature uncomfortable just so you can save on your energy bills.** In the wintertime, ensure your customers can stay warm. In the summer, make sure they can stay cool. Your job is to make them feel at home while they're with you. They should be free from shivering or breaking a sweat while they're experiencing your brand.

# Idea #39

**Take photos of your happy clients (with their permission) and adorn your office walls with them.** Pictures of other folks who have successfully navigated your process will have a calming effect on your future customers who see them. Seeing the smiles will instill confidence that you can get the job done with minimal pain or headache.

**Examples:** Happy kids holding their new toothbrush in dental offices, new car owners in the dealerships, and new babies next to the OB/GYN reception desk.

# Idea #40

**If appropriate, have toys, books, and puzzles in your waiting room.** Both parents and children appreciate having the distraction. If your office is a little more highbrow, simply keep the toys in a nice chest and offer them only when children are present, rather than leaving the toys out at all times. Waiting rooms are not ideal places for high-energy children, so even having these things available for staff to hand out can go a long way toward making everyone's visit a more comfortable experience.

# Idea #41

**Always offer fresh, high-quality coffee or tea.** Make sure it's good. It's this kind of touch that shows you care about your customers. You might also want to offer bottled water for those who don't care for coffee or tea. There is nothing worse than a company that cares so little about its customers that it makes them wait in a cramped waiting room with battery acid for coffee. The right beverage, at the right time, can have a very calming effect (even if it has caffeine).

# Idea #42

**Reassess your office hours.** What do your clients want? (Hint: Ask them.) When are the shops around you open? While it depends on your industry, you may want to stay open past five so folks who don't have the opportunity to visit during the day may do so after work. Certainly, there is a balance to be struck between managing a store and the business to support it being open during those hours. A sure sign that a business is in trouble is when it cuts back its hours. A thriving business would be looking to expand hours—not reduce them.

# Idea #43

**Make your grand opening successful** by:

- ☑ scheduling it during high-traffic times (if your location allows for it),

- ☑ throwing a big grand opening sale,

- ☑ offering food (make this appropriate to the clientele you are seeking),

- ☑ providing a tent for seating outside,

- ☑ direct mailing the local market,

- ☑ offering demonstrations of products or services, and

- ☑ inviting all local business owners, press, and the local chamber of commerce for the ribbon-cutting.

# Idea #44

**Display artwork for sale from local artists.** In doing so, you support the local artist community, gain word-of-mouth through the artists, and bring more interest to your walls. This can be done by writing up an offer and presenting it to a local art gallery. You may want to bring focus to the display either by centering on a specific artist or by having the showing coincide with a particular (and appropriate) event.

# Idea #45

**Create an aromatic environment by using vaporizers or oils.** Have you ever walked past a restaurant or café and been captured by the rich or appetizing aroma wafting from inside? Studies have shown that customers linger longer in aromatic environments. Our sense of smell is the only sense that isn't filtered by the brain. (It bypasses the limbic system entirely.) What can you do to appeal to this sense? What scent might coincide with your branding effort?

**Better:** Coffee and cookies are better than air fresheners. Many people may be allergic (or think they are—same thing) if the wrong scents are used. Some offices ban their use.

# EVENT IDEAS

From fund-raisers to employee appreciation events, this section contains ideas on what an organization can do to bring people together. In bringing people together for one common purpose, we create community. The folks who collectively take part in any event are all sharing that common thread. **Events can be a powerful way to bring value to your community, as well as a great vehicle for marketing your brand.** When you produce an event, attendees bond with your brand in two ways. First, they obviously bond with each other, but second—and more subtly—they bond with you as their host. Now, you may feel that if they're networking with each other, they're not being mindful of you, but as memories and connections are made around your event, your own brand recognition is strengthened in the minds and hearts of those who have attended. Events can be a powerful way to strengthen your brand and bring value to your community.

# Idea #46

**Whether a holiday or a "client appreciation" party**, getting your clients together in the same room and collectively thanking them for their loyal patronage can help you make clients (and friends) for life. Depending on the nature of the organization you operate, you may also have key staff members available to assist with mingling and mixing.

**Variation:** If you have a large organization, you may separate the employee party from the client party, but certainly both are worth having. Employee parties offer the opportunity for internal marketing; client parties, external.

# Idea #47

**Host and promote a competition.** You can call it "The Great _____ Race." Set up a small number of teams, each with a small number of participants. One team wins upon accomplishing the appropriate task you set before them. The entry fee may be the cost (or reduced cost) of your service. The grand prize can be more of your product or service, or you may find a sponsor to provide the prize(s) in exchange for promotion through the event. There are also services available that help you offer some of the larger packages like cars, electronics, and so on. (Essentially, you buy insurance against the cost of the prize if someone wins.)

**Variation:** Donate your product or service to a charitable cause in the winner's name.

# Idea #48

**Hold a children's art sale.** It may be as simple as having a local class draw on gift bags then selling those original artwork pieces to raise funds to sponsor a needy family for Christmas.

**Better:** A less labor-intensive way to get the same thing done would be to scan the artwork, and then create iron-on transfers of it. This allows you to sell more copies of each piece, realize greater profits, and maintain happier artists (and parents.)

# Idea #49

**Hold a Community Day.** Offer your goods or services to your local community at a free or reduced cost. Work with other local businesses and the media to promote your event. This is a great way to give back to the community and bring in new customers who have not visited your business yet. It is also a great way to get to know your neighbors. Work with them to make Community Day a larger event, offering even more value to the community!

# Idea #50

**A restaurant might have a cooking contest for newly graduated local chefs.** During the event, the restaurant would charge ten dollars per person to sample all the showcased dishes. Attendees must vote on which dish is the best. The dish that wins gets on the menu (which should tell the story about how the dish came to be). To make the stakes higher, the restaurant might even hire the winning chef.

**Tip:** This idea also works when you need an event catered and don't have a large budget.

# Idea #51

**Conduct a window display contest** (instead of a sidewalk sale). Make voter cards available, and encourage participants to vote on their favorite display. Offer free samples to entice voters to try your product or service. Maintain a guestbook to track traffic and build your contact database.

## Idea #52

**Participate in a local gallery hop,** where local artists bring their wares to display at a collection of stores and businesses. Maps of participating businesses are provided, and the event is advertised throughout the community. Businesses may serve appetizers and beverages to visitors on the tour, and artists may be present to talk about their work. This may be done for free (for the exposure, sharing the expense for printing the maps, posters, and so on), or you might charge a small cover as the maps are handed out. (You would charge hoppers only once—not at each location.)

# Idea #53

**Just because you provide a service instead of a product, it doesn't mean you can't participate in sidewalk sales.** Use sidewalk sales to:

- ☑ Get to know your neighborhood and its foot traffic.

- ☑ Educate the public on what you do.

- ☑ Survey the public for what they want. Get suggestions and ideas from people on what they need and how you may best provide it.

- ☑ Conduct free demonstrations of your product or service.

**Tip:** Don't worry if you don't have a sidewalk. Find out when the next big local sidewalk sale is, and work out an arrangement with one of the participating vendors (one that compliments your own offerings would be preferred) to share its space.

# Idea #54

**A number of good causes offer a "lockup" program to enlist members of the community in raising funds.** The idea is to publicize a mock arrest and jailing (though you may really be handcuffed and driven to the local jail in a police car) in exchange for "bail" (contributions to the cause). The "arrestee" then contacts the members of his own network to solicit for a set amount of funds in return for his freedom. Once bail has been made, you're set free. If you can't be away from your job, there's often a "house arrest" option. Sign yourself up, and publicize it as widely as you can. You're gaining a life experience, a wonderful story, and good karma.

# Idea #55

**Host an adult spelling-bee competition to help raise money for your cause.** Much like a walk-a-thon, participants are called upon to gather donations from their support network, based on the number of words they spell correctly, as opposed to donating so much money for each mile walked. Conduct the event on a weekend or evening so kids can attend and see adults sweating in the spotlight.

**Tip:** Pull in community leaders to make things more interesting. They will also lend wonderful support to the event.

# Idea #56

**Offer an adult education class or seminar.** This may be something you conduct through a local school or university, or it could be offered through a local business association or group. Your intent is to bring value to the attendees and the program hosts and to become known.

**Variation:** Spread the wealth. Invite other professionals in the area to speak as well. By doing so, you offer more value to the seminar and improve your referral network. Other professionals will also be able to help in the marketing of the seminar by reaching out to their own networks.

**Variation:** Find a professional or celebrity speaker, and bring him in to talk about a topic that is relevant to your audience. Partner with a local hotel and business associations to provide the venue and help cover the costs.

# EVENT PROMOTION

You've determined you're going to have an event, and by now, you know what it is going to be. Now what? **How do you get the word out?** This section provides you with ideas and tips for publicizing your event so that it can be successful.

## Idea #57

**People love to hear great music,** so if you would like to offer music at your next event, make sure the band is well-known and worth your audience's attention. Nothing screams cheap like bad or inappropriate music that is forced upon would-be customers. Your band should understand your business and your clientele and be able to produce music that fits. If you pick the right band, adding it to the list of cool things to see and do at your event will be a draw.

# Idea #58

**Contact your local TV and/or radio stations about teaming up** to produce special events and programming around your issue. You and your partner stations might consider creating news stories on key issues in the community, while also sponsoring city hall forums, fairs, and other outreach events. The goal of partnering with your local broadcasters is to extend the value of 1.) your outreach efforts and 2.) their programming.

# Ideas #59–66

**Don't skimp on the small stuff when you're producing an event.** People will always expect certain things, and if they've paid to be there, they have a right to expect those things.

💡 **#59: If you have an event or seminar, provide beverages, a coat rack, and snacks.**

💡 **#60: Validate parking if free parking isn't available.** If you can't validate parking, work out an arrangement with your venue to include parking in the price of admission.

💡 **#61: If parking is still an issue, offer a shuttle service to and from the event.**

💡 **#62: Make it easy for people to register; offer online registration from your website.** This method should collect their contact information, accept and process credit cards, and send attendees their confirmation automatically. (There are services available for accomplishing this if you're not sure how to do it yourself.)

💡 **#63: Make sure the bathrooms are clean** and tended to regularly.

☀ **#64: Ensure there are enough trash** receptacles and that they are emptied periodically (before they're overflowing).

☀ **#65: Work with your local chamber of commerce**, business associations, and networking organizations to promote your event to their members.

☀ **#66: Offer meals during an all-day event.** This serves two purposes. First, you'll have less stragglers wandering back in from lunch after the event has picked back up. Second, by giving attendees a reason to sit at their table, they network with each other over lunch, bonding with each other (and your brand) in the process.

# MEDIA RELATIONS

**One of the best ways to promote an idea, event, or yourself is to build a relationship with your local media.** Free press can be granted to you through newspaper, television, radio, and the Internet if you've taken the time to foster those relationships, or if you can bring value to media efforts and the local community. This section provides tips on working with your local media to bring awareness to your cause through press releases, public service announcements, editorials, interviews, and more.

# Idea #67

**A great way to get your organization's name into the local community is to sponsor or underwrite a local news program, whether television or radio.** Make sure the media station (and format) you select is appropriate for your target market. For instance, if you're looking to reach an older crowd, maybe you want to advertise on an "oldies" radio station, which plays songs that were hits in the past. If you want to reach the younger generation, you might look at a Top 40 or hip-hop radio station. If you're looking for a sports-oriented crowd, you'll want to place your ad in front of the folks sitting at home, watching the sports channels.

**Tip:** An ideal place to advertise is with talk-radio programs. National Public Radio (NPR) and similar "talk-based" formats offer an audience that is already tuned into the discussion, rather than an audience that will be annoyed by another ad that separates them from their music. Underwriting these programs on a local level will also provide you with the opportunity to support a wonderful service in your own community.

# Idea #68

**A news or press release about a new program or event is a wonderful way to inform the local media and its audience about your latest efforts.** Before you do this, however, you must know exactly what your intent is for your news release. Make sure you can answer the following questions:

- ☑ Who am I trying to reach?
- ☑ What is my message?
- ☑ What am I trying to accomplish by providing this message? (For example, are you trying to educate, motivate to take action, or persuade?)
- ☑ Why should the community care?

Once you've answered these questions, you are ready to begin crafting your release. Below is a brief list of steps to take. We have also provided you a news/press release template and sample to assist you in building your own news release at

http://ideas.dreamscapemultimedia.com/idea -center/media-relations.html.

## Basic Format of a News Release

☑ Print the release on your organization's letterhead.

☑ Type "For Immediate Release" and the date along the upper-left or upper-right margin.

☑ Directly across from "For Immediate Release," include the label "Contact for Reporters" and place your contact person's name, phone number, and e-mail address below.

☑ Next, clearly describe the news event with a short, compelling headline. Center your headline on the page, and display it in bold font. Then, position a short sentence below the headline to summarize the release, and type it in italics or bold font, using a smaller font size.

☑ Begin the first paragraph with your dateline. The dateline identifies where the news originated. Following the dateline, give a one- or two-sentence summary for your press or news release. Include the date, time, and other time-critical information related to your activities. Concisely summarize the who, what, when, where, and why. For example:

*Lansing, Michigan* – Best-selling author Matt Schoenherr discusses marketing strategies at a two-day Culture of Success event beginning Wednesday, December 12, 2012, at Madison Square Garden in New York City. Tickets for the event sold out during the first week of sales.

☑ In the second paragraph, provide a quote from a leader or key person within your organization. The leader quoted should be closely connected with the event, and his role should be clearly identified.

Note: Ensure all quotes add value to your story. Limit the number of quotes captured in your release to one or two people.

☑ Type -more- at the bottom of the first page if your release goes beyond one page. Limit your news or press release to no more than two pages; one page is preferred.

☑ The third paragraph may contain additional details on the event or program, as well as information on its history. This is also the place to include contact information for those who are interested in learning more.

☑ Finally, end your release with information about your company or organization. You can also do the same for a partner or sponsor; however, if you want to list more than two, avoid placing them here. Instead, include the list as a separate attachment. Your goal is to make the news release easy to read and digest for reporters and editors.

☑ Finally, typing ### or -30- at the very end indicates the end of the copy.

## General Guidelines

☑ Use short, explanatory sentences.

☑ Avoid the use of jargon. Explain any acronyms at their first appearance, such as, "Public service announcements (PSAs)."

☑ Avoid glorifying or demonizing within your release. Your goal is to report news without driving public opinion about it. Avoid judgment words like "very," "thrilling," "massive," and so on. Your descriptions should be as objective as the lens of a camera.

☑ Link the facts of the project or event to an important issue or need in your local community. Using real-life examples helps make the human connection. Highlight benefits of your work to the community.

☑ Review for clarity and flow, and ensure all words and names are spelled correctly.[1]

## Idea #69

**Offer to be available for comment or interviews on your effort.** Television or radio news programs are always interested in talking with local experts who can speak to the issues faced by the community, especially during rush-hour radio broadcasts or early morning/late evening TV programming. The broader your topic, the more appealing you will be to these news producers. Contact program producers or hosts, and offer your contribution. If they like your eloquence and topic, they'll gladly put you in front of their audience.

# Idea #70

**Consider approaching your local media stations (radio, television, newspaper) to discuss the possibility of a partnership to raise community awareness on your issue or industry.** With the right spin, you will be able to broaden the awareness in your local market while also sponsoring community discussion at city council meetings, festivals, and other community events. In joining forces, you bring value to each other; your outreach efforts are improved, and the value and local impact of their programming is increased.

# Idea #71

Often, radio stations will set aside time in their news schedules for taking public comment on important issues. **Begin by calling the news directors of your local radio stations and asking for the chance to offer your editorial comment.** (Make sure you have a good sense as to whether they cater to the audience you want to reach.) Focus on local concerns related to your work.

# Idea #72

Especially if you're a nonprofit, **public service announcement (PSAs) can go a long way to getting the word out about your latest effort.** PSAs are often aired on local radio and TV stations, and often placed in newspapers. They often raise awareness of topics important to their audience through funny, emotional, or compelling thirty- to ninety-second productions. As long as the announcement has benefit to the public, and as long as it's not gratuitous self-promotion, the media agency will likely mention it to their audience.

**Example:** "That's Public Health" PSA (approximately fifteen seconds)

*Ever have a vaccination? That's public health.*

*Expect the water from your tap to be safe? That's public health.*

*Ever taken your baby to a clinic for a checkup? That's public health.*

*Think public health has never touched your life?*

*Think again.*

*A message from _____* [2]

# SURVEYS AND DETERMINING ROI*

**Many folks don't know they are supposed to track the return on their invested marketing dollars.** Those who do have an idea they're supposed to do this usually aren't sure where to begin. Many struggle with advertising here or there, and end up never knowing what has worked and what hasn't or why. Eventually, they begin to develop advertising apathy. They're frustrated that sales aren't going the way they want, they're out of ideas, and they're unsure about how to proceed—or even if they should proceed! By using surveys and other means of testing for market response to your efforts, you can begin to shed light on your effectiveness.

*ROI - Return on Investment

# Idea #73

**If you aren't doing so already, casually survey all clients before they cash out.** Kindly request their permission to ask them basic questions about their occupation, their use of time, the reason why they're in front of you, what they like (and would improve) about their experience, and so on. This will give you a better idea of who comes to your store and why. Train your staff to do the same. Ask the same questions of everyone.

**Tip:** You don't have to ask a flurry of questions from every customer that walks through your doors. Ask a single question of every customer one week, another question the next, and so on, and you will begin to shape a picture about the people who shop from you.

# Idea #74

**Exit interviews are a must anytime you have an employee submit his resignation.** In conducting this survey, you begin to determine where you're falling short in keeping your people. Often, you'll find that money isn't the top issue. What you're looking for is how you are able to improve your internal marketing. How do you craft a culture that keeps and nurtures the best employees? How do you build fierce loyalty and pride among your employees? Among your customers? Your vendors? Begin asking the tough questions. The sooner you get the answers, the sooner you'll be able to emerge as a company people aspire to work for and with.

# Idea #75

**Mystery shop your competition.** Mystery shopping is shopping with your competition, under the cover of anonymity, with the intent of seeing how they perform. Consider this marketplace espionage. While much less direct than simply introducing yourself and swapping stories about successes and follies, this still gives you vital information about what they're doing, how they're doing it, and how you may better leverage your own efforts.

**Better:** Pay someone to mystery shop you. Look for the good, the bad, and the ugly. Act on what you discover.

**Variation:** While there are professional mystery-shopping organizations widely available, there is another way. Seek out strategic partners within your network, and arrange to have them shop you. Tutor them on the facets of the customer experience you would like to know most about. This may even be a reciprocal effort, where you shop them in return.

**Tip:** You must remain open to criticism if you're going to have yourself shopped. Being closed-minded to the results may render them useless and leave you in the dark.

# Idea #76

After some time working with clients, **provide them with a survey** to get a feeling for how you're doing. This can be delivered back to you electronically or by mail. Keep it short. Five or six carefully crafted questions can offer valuable feedback on ways to improve your business practices. At the end of the survey, reaffirm that all their information is private and confidential. They need to know you won't break their trust.

**Variation:** Make sure to state that they also have the option of providing their name and permission to use their words in your marketing efforts. In doing so, you may find yourself with some nice testimonials.

# MARKETING COLLATERAL

**Many folks don't know they are supposed to track the return on their invested marketing dollars.** Here are some things to keep in mind when considering your brand signatures, such as your logo, brochures, business cards, websites, and so on. Your marketing materials are not to be confused with your brand! Branding is a phenomenon that occurs in the mind of the consumer. Branding is not a logo or catchy tagline; these are expressions of the brand. You must take the expression of your brand seriously, for a badly managed brand can erode your image in the marketplace. Ensure your marketing materials are up to par—every time. If it is questionable whether a certain piece of marginal collateral should be used, it is best to not use it.

# Idea #77

**How long have you had your current logo?**
Does it still reflect the culture of your
organization? Does it still reflect the promise of
your brand? Is it time to recreate it?

**Remember:** Reinventing yourself is a
marketable event, which—if it's done well—can
help you shed some negative feelings or
associations your brand might have picked up
along the way.

## Idea #78

**If you must have a brochure, have it professionally created.** Describe the problem and your solution, and include your customers' testimonials. Avoid technical jargon. Use bulleted lists to enhance readability. Use appropriate graphics to enhance visual appeal.

# Idea #79

**Consider the signage at your office or facility.** Can a visitor find you easily? Can he find his way around your facility easily? Large buildings such as hospitals, office buildings, and malls often suffer from poor signage, creating a sense of unease and annoyance in their patrons. You know that even grocery stores can benefit from clear signage if you've ever had the misfortune of searching for way too long to locate a certain item on your grocery list.

# Idea #80

**Send greeting cards** to mark social events, such as holidays, wedding anniversaries, or birthdays. This adds a personal touch that will be remembered.

**Tip 1:** Too busy to fill out all the cards? Hire it out. These services are available.

**Tip 2:** You know those custom cards you had printed out? If you had left them blank, they could have become all-purpose, and could have easily fulfilled these applications as well.

# Idea #81

**Purchase thank-you cards, and send them to your clients,** thanking them for their business, patience, and so on. Make sure your company logo is on the card somewhere. Include your business card inside.

**Variation 1:** Fill out the cards by hand. Doing so adds a more personal touch.

**Variation 2:** Send a thank-you card on their first-year anniversary as your client or for another notable milestone.

# Idea #82

A great rule for a brochure is, "If you can't say it all on a business card, you shouldn't say it at all." (Okay, so it's not really a rule, but it should be.) **Distill what you want to say about your product or service and fit it on a business card.** Leave off your contact information; that's what your actual business card is for. Instead, list a few bullet points with the message you are trying to convey, and add some nice, simple graphics. By doing this, you are able to leave those you meet with a message that they can carry with them or organize into their Rolodex. (This presumes you made a great enough impact to compel them to keep your business card.)

**Example:** This idea is currently used by Dreamscape Multimedia with great success. (In fact, as far as we know, we invented the concept.) We place the tagline on the front of the card, and the content on the back, for a playing card–type feel. Also, by utilizing both front and back in your design, you can leave two cards on a bulletin board or elsewhere, flipping one over to create a small, two-piece brochure/billboard effect.

# Idea #83

**The best and most obvious reason for visiting some tables at trade shows is for the free giveaways.** You will find that many people will make the rounds to collect the free stuff. In some cases, the booths without free giveaways may experience lower traffic as a result. It's a cheap ploy, but the right giveaway can gain you exposure you wouldn't have had without it. Of course, you have to question the quality of your traffic if it's only coming over to steal another one of those great metal pens…

**Tip:** You can have fun with your giveaways. After all, if it's really good, it will likely end up in the hands of their kids.

# Idea #84

**Why is it you occasionally see billboards that attempt to be brochures?** Is their message so important that it couldn't possibly be distilled down into a couple brief phrases? Is their key message so complex? When you get ready to make your billboard investment, don't insist your billboard become more than a billboard. A message received from a billboard is geared toward the audience on the go—and they're usually going over 70 miles per hour. Keep it eye-catching, short, and simple for greatest impact.

# Idea #85

Do you have a client who just had a birthday, anniversary, or baby? **Send flowers, balloons, gift or wine baskets, or something else that creatively says, "Congratulations!"** It makes a big impression on the recipient, and who doesn't like to be remembered during these times?

**Tip:** This works with employees as well. Remember: There's the external marketing you do to bring in more business, but there's also the internal marketing you do to increase morale, loyalty, and productivity.

# Idea #86

**Use the Fortune Cookie Effect.** Engage your customers with a collection of cute or hidden messages in your packaging. Chocolates, fortune cookies, ketchup and beer are just some of the products that have successfully used this technique for drawing interest to their branding. The idea is to embed a message into your merchandising to inspire interest and conversation around the message—and therefore the product and, finally, the brand.

**Story:** When my wife was five months pregnant with our first baby, medical experts told her he was measuring small, and that it was possible he had stopped growing, which of course lent itself to scary self-talk about a myriad potential birth defects. During the course of that day, she was given a Dove chocolate, which came wrapped in purple foil and contained a message inside, as they all do. This message said, "There is greatness in smallness." The timing being perfect, we took it as a sign, and it helped us relax.

Of course, the happy ending is that the next time she went in for an ultrasound, everything measured fine, and we're pleased to say that our boy is a happy, healthy, and complete individual. The foil wrapper has been glued to a magnet and now resides on our refrigerator.

That little piece of marketing by Dove will now be a part of our family story for many years.

This can be the power of the Fortune Cookie Effect.

# Idea #87

Many a cheap diaper has been bought because of commercials showing it can hold the contents of an entire water balloon. **Whether at trade shows or in your TV ads or videos, demonstrations prove your products work.** This is why those late-night infomercials are so successful. Even brochures can illustrate a step-by-step series of images that prove success.

What can you do to illustrate your product in action?

# Idea #88

How often are you bringing value to your clients? **Offer a regular newsletter, article, or column.** Ensure that whatever you put out maintains a consistent look and feel with the rest of your image; this assists you in furthering the development of your brand.

**Better:** You should be collecting the e-mail addresses of everyone who comes to you. Reduce your printing costs, save trees, and extend your reach by offering your network an e-newsletter.

# Idea #89

**Collect testimonials from your best clients as a regular part of your follow-up survey process.** Make sure you tell them you'll be using all or part of their testimonials in your ongoing marketing efforts. Then, incorporate the best testimonials into every touch you have with your clients, such as invoices and marketing collateral (newsletters, ads, and so on). Remember: If you say it about you, it's bragging; if someone else says it about you, it's true.

**Tip:** Do you have a stellar client who would love to write you a testimonial but is always extremely busy? Offer to write it for her, and tell her if she approves, she may simply sign off on it. This allows you to mention the important stuff. The best testimonials state:

» the problem the client was having,
» why the client chose you,
» what you did for the client, and
» why others should choose you.

# Idea #90

What's better than putting a written testimonial into your brochure? **Video testimonials delivered on your website.** Now your happiest clients can communicate face-to-face with your future prospects, anytime, anywhere. In a sales presentation and a client asks about a problem you know your video testimonial addresses? "Well, Mr./Mrs. Customer, you bring up a good point. It just so happens we also have another client who went through the process you're describing, and he was infinitely pleased with the results he received from us. Let me show you what he said."

**Tip:** Use the testimonial in your next television ad, and get more mileage out of your video.

# Idea #91

**Send reminders to refresh your clients' memory of specific recurring events,** such as dental appointments or subscription renewals. If you're using direct mail (postcards, letters, and so on), have your clients fill out the address information for their next reminder at the time of checkout.

**Tip:** Go one step further and hand them a sticker with the date of their next appointment, for easy placement in their wall calendars.

**Example:** Oil-change shops are great at this. They are always certain to leave those little window clings on your windshield for easy reference. As a result, you always know exactly when you're due for a visit!

**Better:** Send them their calendar appointment electronically. (You *are* collecting their e-mail addresses, right?)

# Idea #92

**Videotape your event.**

**Step 1:** Get quotes from people at several of the local video shops, interview them, and look at their portfolios. Pick the one that you feel best about.

**Step 2:** Have them videotape your seminar and make it web-ready. Ask them to send you all raw and edited footage. You should have this in case you want to use it later.

**Step 3:** Have your video folks send the finished product to your web designer/developer so the video may be added to your website.

**Step 4:** Put the video in a secure place on your website, and ask visitors to register for the free information. Collect their e-mail addresses for future e-newsletter mailings!

**Step 5:** Repeat.

# Idea #93

The information on your stationery, business cards, thank-you cards, websites, e-mail signatures, order forms, direct mail pieces, invoices, packing slips, and all other correspondence **should include your company name, address, phone numbers, fax numbers, and website address.** Your goal at all times is to make it easy for your customers to do business with you.

# Idea #94

**Using color can be a powerful tool.** It engages us, helps establish brand identities and market products, and increases our memory of the brand. The colors we choose to use with our branding efforts carry with them certain iconic qualities. For instance, the color white tends to symbolize purity and innocence. In Western cultures, white is the color for brides, but in Eastern cultures, white symbolizes death. Similarly, the color black tends to translate to mystery, elegance, and sophistication. In Western cultures, black symbolizes mourning. Pay close attention to the colors you use in your marketing collateral.

# Idea #95

When your business is the first one that comes to mind as a place to find a product or service, you have achieved what is called top-of-mind awareness. Top-of-mind awareness is built and reinforced through repetition.

If you hold a retail store, 85 percent of your customers live or work within a five-mile radius of your business. When driving to and from work, school, and shopping, they pass your location some fifty to sixty times a month. **Your sign should be designed so that it commands their attention every time they pass.**

That's how signs help build top-of-mind awareness and brand your business. To further this effort, make sure your sign is included as part of your overall marketing strategy.

# Ideas #96–101

**When getting ready to host a booth at a trade show,** once you know the size and area dimensions you'll be working with, the next step is deciding what information and content you want to display. Here are some tips:

- ♀ **#96: Your company name and logo must be visible.** If visitors don't know who and what the display is about in a matter of five seconds or less, their interest will be lost. The company's name and logo should be easy to see. Remember: Always include your website address.

- ♀ **#97: Don't make the overall design too distracting.** Too much information and clutter will create confusion. Neatness, simplicity, and visibility are some of the most important aspects. Images should be crisp and professional-looking—no low-resolution images. All content should be appropriate and pertain to the rest of the display.

- ♀ **#98: For maximum impact, use color to make a statement, and let your display pop out.** Color schemes can help set a specific mood or tone. Pick colors that will correlate with your company's tone and theme.

**#99: Successful trade show booths make it easy for visitors to retrieve information.** Pass out flyers or business cards. Consider creating interactive displays, such as games, contests, drawings, or giveaways. Think of anything that will get the visitors intrigued and involved. This is a great way to add some flair to your display!

**#100:** Prior to a big day of participating in a local trade show, **make sure you've e-mailed your customers and prospects to let them know** 1. of the trade show (in case they hadn't heard) and 2. of your participation in it. A short e-mail broadcast is a quick, easy, and low-cost way of promoting both the trade show and yourself. The more people who turn out for the trade show, the greater its success; likewise, the more people who stop by your booth, the greater the chance for your success.

**#101: Say thank you.** Show your appreciation for those who have taken the time to stop by your booth and engage you (when they could have invested their time elsewhere among the hundreds of other booths). This should be viewed as a critical part of your follow-up strategy and can be done over the phone, via e-mail or direct mail, or through a face-to-face visit afterward—

just do it. The most powerful showing of gratitude is delivered in person.

# References

1  National Association of County & City Health Officials (2006). Writing a News Release. Retrieved August 29, 2010, from http://www.naccho.org/advocacy/marketing/guide/news.cfm

2  National Association of County & City Health Officials (2006). Public Service Announcements Template. Retrieved August 29, 2010, from http://www.naccho.org/advocacy/marketing/upload/PSA_TEMPLATE.doc

## About the Author

Matthew J. Schoenherr is a husband, father of four, business owner, and marketing consultant. As the author of *Ideas,* he continues his work in supporting the worthy goals of service and commerce in the business and nonprofit communities. Matt crafted *Ideas* to help jump-start sales and branding efforts while improving marketing literacy through a format that is no-nonsense, easy to read and easy to implement.

## About Dreamscape Multimedia

Dreamscape Multimedia is a full-service web design and marketing clearinghouse offering web design, web hosting, branding and marketing services for small businesses and nonprofits.

## Special Thanks

Thank you to the following people who provided ideas, inspiration and correction along the way: Kelly Schoenherr-Gram, Chuck Gifford, Jack Pyle, John Meatte, Tom Donaldson, Dennis Wrobleski, Bob Parsons, Christopher Niem Henley and Yvonne LeFave.

## For More Information

For more marketing brilliance, see Matt's website at www.mattschoenherr.com.

**DREAMSCAPE**
MULTIMEDIA

www.ingramcontent.com/pod-product-compliance
Lightning Source LLC
Chambersburg PA
CBHW022042210326
41458CB00080B/6604/J